Messiah's Handbook

Messiah's Handbook

Reminders
for the
Advanced Soul

Jacket design: © Cygnus Books 2006, 01550 777 701

Printed by Cambrian Printers
www.cambrian-printers.co.uk

Foreword

The last time I saw the *Messiah's Handbook* was when I threw it away.

I had been using it as I was taught in *Illusions:* hold question in mind, close eyes, open handbook at random, pick left page or right. Eyes open, read answer.

Always before it worked: fear dissolved in a smile, doubt lifted by sudden understanding. Always had I been charmed and entertained by what these pages had to tell me.

So that dark day I opened the book, trusting. "Why did my friend Donald Shimoda, who had so much to teach that we so needed to learn, why did he have to die such a senseless death?"

Eyes open, listen to the answer:

Everything in this book may be wrong.

A burst of night and rage, I remember, instant fury. I turn to it for help and *this* is my answer? I threw the book as hard and as far from me as I could, pages fluttering above that nameless Iowa hayfield, the thing tumbling slow motion, shuddering forever down toward the weeds. I didn't watch to see where it fell.

I flew from that field and never flew back. The handbook, that senseless hurtful agony-page, was gone.

Twenty years later came a package to a writer in care of the publisher. In the package a note:

Dear Richard Bach, I found this when I was plowing my dad's soybean field. The field's a quarter-section used to be in hay and he told me you landed there once with the guy they killed they said was magic. So this has been plowed under I guess for a long time else it's been disked and harrowed every year and nobody's seen it till now. For all that, it's not much hurt and I figured it's your property and if you're still alive you ought to have it.

No return address. On the pages, my own finger-prints in engine oil from an old Fleet biplane, a sifting of coarse dusts, a stem or two of grass falling out when I fanned it open.

Rage gone, I held the book a long time, remembering.

Everything in this book may be wrong. Sure enough. But everything may be right, as well. Right and wrong's not up to a book. I'm the only one to say what's true for me. I'm responsible.

I leafed through the pages, wondering. Is the book returned to me the same one I threw away, so long ago? Had it been resting quietly underground or had it been changing to become what some future reader needed to remember?

At last, eyes closed, I held the handbook once more and asked.

Dear strange mystical volume, why did you come back?

Riffled the pages for a moment, opened my eyes and saw.

*E*very person,
all the events of your life,
are there because you have drawn them there.

*W*hat you choose to do with them
is up to you.

I smiled, reading that. And I chose, this time, instead of throwing it away, to keep the *Messiah's Handbook*.

And I choose now, instead of wrapping it in silence, to let you unwrap the whole of it and listen to its whisper for yourself, whenever you wish.

Some of the ideas I've found in this book I've said in others: There are words here from *Illusions* and *One* and *Jonathan Livingston Seagull* and *Out of My Mind* and *The Ferret Chronicles*. A writer's life, like a reader's, is fiction and fact; it's almost-happened and half-remembered and once-dreamed. The smallest part of our being is history that somebody else can verify.

Yet fiction and reality are friends; the only way to tell some truths is in the language of stories.

Donald Shimoda, for instance, my reluctant Messiah, is a real person, though as far as I know he's never had a mortal body or a voice that anyone else could hear. So is Stormy Ferret real, flying her miniature transport through a terrible storm because she believes in her mission; so is Harley Ferret throwing himself into a midnight sea to save his friend; so are all these characters real who have brought me to life.

Enough explaining. Before you may take a handbook home, however, test this copy, be sure it works.

Hold a question in mind, please. Now close your eyes, open the handbook at random and pick left page or right,

—*Richard Bach*

*C*louds don't worry about
     falling into the sea because
     they can't (a) fall or (b) drown.
But they are free
to believe they can,
      and they may fear
       if they wish.

$\mathcal{M}$ost happy, successful people
at one time
have considered suicide.
They decided against it.

*Y*ou are free to create
and honor
whatever past you choose,
to heal and transform
your present.

*Y*our harshest truths are dreams, and your gentlest dreams are true.

*E*verything is exactly as it is for a reason.
The crumb on your table is
no mystical reminder of this morning's cookie,
it is there because you have
chosen not to remove it.
No exceptions.

*J*ust because somebody drops in
on you from another dimension,
don't assume they're wiser than you
about anything at all, or
that they can do anything better
than you can do it yourself.

*D*iscarnate or mortal,
what matters about people is
what they know.

*E*verybody came here with a
Design-O-Life Personal Future Construction Kit.
Not everybody remembers
where they put it.

*L*ife tells you nothing,
        it shows you everything.

You've all learned something
that someone somewhere
needs to remember.

How will you let them know?

*L*ean into your fears,
dare them to do their worst
and cut them down when they try.
If you don't, they'll clone themselves,
mushroom till they surround you,
choke the road to the life you want.

*E*very turn you fear
is empty air,
dressed to look
like jagged hell.

*O*ver and again you'll meet
a new theology,
and every time will come the test:
Do I take this belief
to become my life?

*I*f God looked directly into your eyes
and said,

"I command that you be
happy in the world,
as long as you live,"

What would you do?

*I*t's called a default belief,
when you agree to rules
before you think,
when you go along
because you're expected to.
A million of those in a lifetime
unless you're careful.

Life does not require you to be consistent,
cruel, patient, helpful, angry, rational, thoughtless,
loving, rash, open-minded, neurotic, careful, rigid,
tolerant, wasteful, rich, downtrodden, gentle, sick,
considerate, funny, stupid, healthy, greedy, beautiful,
lazy, responsive, foolish, sharing, pressured, intimate,
hedonistic, industrious, manipulative, insightful,
capricious, wise, selfish, kind, or sacrificed.

Life does, however, require you to feel
the consequences of your choices.

What if all these levels inside you
are your friends,
and they know a lot more
than you know?
What if your teachers are here, right now?
Instead of always talking, what if for a change
you listen?

*A*nger is always fear,
      and fear is always fear
of loss.

*R*emember that this world
is not reality.
It's a playground of appearances
on which you practice overcoming seems-to-be
with your knowing of what is.

Want a trouble-free future?
Why did you show up
in spacetime if
you didn't want trouble?

The less you know about the game,
    and the less you remember you're a player,
the more senseless living becomes.

*I*f one inspired innocent loving soaring dreamer
believes in a universe of joy and
light and perfect being,
and if she's wrong and dies,
it's not the dreamer who's been foolish,
but the universe.

*T*here's a reason you chose
what's happening around you.
Hang on, live your way through
the best you know,
and in a bit
you'll find out why.

*T*he highest nation is
a structure of values,
and its patriotism
is conscience.

*E*very turn in your life,
every time you decide,
you become parent
to all your alternate selves who follow.

*A*ny powerful idea
is absolutely fascinating
and absolutely useless
until you decide to put it to work.

When you seek inspiration,
it's ideas you want.
When you pray for guidance,
it's ideas that show the way.
But you have to pay attention!

*P*retend that you honestly

truly deeply want to know

who you are,

where you came from,

and why you're here.

*P*retend you're willing

never to rest till you know.

Now:

Can you imagine yourself

not finding out?

"**B**ad" is that which makes you unhappy. "Evil" is that which makes you *very* unhappy.

*Y*our philosophy is
a way of looking at the universe
that guides you in daily life.
You probably won't find it in textbooks.

The biggest reason
you don't get answers is
that you haven't
asked the questions.

When you pull a propeller
through compression,
don't be surprised
when the engine starts.

*W*hatever you decide to live,
you'll live not once
but a thousand times over,
remembering
for the rest of your life.

Guilt is the tension you feel
to change your past, present, or future
for someone else's sake.
It's your tension, you can let it go.

You know nothing till intuition agrees.

When you dream,
　　　　　　all the scenery, characters,
events, perils, and outcomes are built
from your own consciousness,
　　　the darks and oppressions
　　　　　as well as the delights.

Same with the world awake,
　　　though it takes you longer to build it.

*S*hop for security over happiness
and you buy it, at that price.

How many live lifetimes
without finding what they know and love?
Many.
It's your job to be sure you're not one of 'em.

When the ship of your spirit
hits the reef of matter,
it's the reef
that's smashed to pieces.

*I*f it's never your fault,
you can't take responsibility for it.
If you can't take responsibility for it,
you'll always be its victim.

*Y*our depth of intimacy with another
is inversely proportional
to the number of others in your life.

Humanity isn't a physical description,
it's a spiritual goal.
It's not something you're given,
it's something you earn.

*Y*our highest right
knows all futures.
Listen to its whisper
and find that the prize ahead
is your own greatest happiness.

*I*t's okay to do ordinary,
so long as you don't *feel* ordinary.

$\mathcal{H}$aving climbed certain peaks
you'll descend no more,
but spread your wings and fly beyond.

What's going to happen
has already happened.

What you perceive is up to you.

you will never grow up.

$\mathcal{W}$hy do you think you're odd and different,
a lonely outsider,
when all that's happened is
you haven't found your family?

With every choice
you risk the life you would have had;
with every decision,
you lose it.

*Y*ou build your personal world
calm or wild
according to what you wish.
You can weave peace in the midst of chaos,
you can destroy in the midst of paradise.
Depends on how you shape your spirit.

*F*ind the greatest teachers,

ask the hardest questions,

they never say, "Study philosophy,"

or, "Get your degree."

They say,

"You already know."

*I*t's a slow process,

   changing principles,

      and you'll never know they've changed

         until something that used to be right

   just doesn't feel that way any more.

*U*nconditional love is

no more a force in spacetime

than it is in chess,

or soccer or ice hockey.

Rules define life in games,

and unconditional love

doesn't recognize rules.

*F*orgetting is
what people
on this planet
call "consciousness."

The smallest turn today
will take you
to a dramatically different tomorrow.

What you knew
before you were born
isn't lost.
You only hide it till you're tested,
till it's time to remember.
And sure enough, when you want,
you'll find some odd funny beautiful way
to find it again.

*Y*ou chose us for your teachers?

We chose you, too!

You care about what you're learning?

We care, too!

You think we're in your life

because you love us?

Can't you understand?

*W*e love you, too!

*C*an miles truly separate friends?

If you want to be with one that you love,

aren't you already there?

*F*orget about faith.

　　　　You don't need faith to fly,
　　　you need to understand flying.

When you learn
what this world is,
how it works,
you automatically start getting miracles . . .
what others will call miracles.

*y*ou are the game-playing,
               fun-having creatures;
you are the otters of the universe.

Spacetime is a fairly primitive school.
But a lot of folks stay with the belief of it
even when it's boring,
and they don't want the lights turned on early.

*L*ike attracts like.

Be who you are,
calm and clear and bright,
asking yourself every minute
is this what I really want to do,
doing it only when you answer yes.

*T*his turns away those who have
nothing to learn from who you are
and attracts those who do,
and from whom you have to learn as well.

"Just your imagination?"

Of course it's your imagination!

This world is your imagination.

Have you forgotten?

You do not exist to impress the world.
You exist to live your life
in a way that will make you happy.

*A*ny different spacetime is a dream
for a good sane earthling,
which you are going to be
for a little while yet.

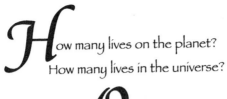

How many lives on the planet?
How many lives in the universe?

One.

*T*here are grand rewards for those
who pick the high hard roads,
but those rewards are hidden by years.
Every choice is made in the uncaring blind,
no guarantees from the world around you.

*N*o matter how qualified or deserving you are,
you will never reach a better life
until you can imagine it for yourself,
and allow yourself to have it.

You build the appearances around you.
You get exactly what you deserve.

Who's to blame,
who's to credit, but you?
Who can change it, any time you wish,
but you?

*Y*our only obligation in any lifetime
is to be true to yourself.

*I*s this my highest sense of right?
Is this the direction I want most to go?
Is this the way in which I can give my greatest gift?

There aren't just a few of you
   scattered through the land
      who are creatures of light
and everyone else is a lump of clay.
      You're all light-beings.

*R*eality has nothing to do with appearances,
with your narrow way of seeing.
Reality is love expressed,
pure perfect love,
unbrushed by space and time.

As you're one with the person you were
a second ago or a week ago,
as you're one with the person you're going to be
a moment from now or a week from now,
so you're one with the person you were a lifetime ago,
the one you are in an alternate lifetime,
the one you'll be a hundred lifetimes
into what you call your future.

The choice to follow any real adventure
is measured by this view:
When you look back on it,
will you be glad you dared,
or glad you didn't?

*T*o love someone unconditionally
is not to care who they are or what they do.

*U*nconditional love, on the surface,
looks the same as indifference.

Hatred is love without the facts.
Why tell lies to separate
and destroy yourselves
when the truth is
you're one?

*Y*ou have the freedom to be yourself,
your true self, here and now,
and nothing can stand in your way.

$\mathcal{N}$o one does anything uncharacteristic
of who they are.

*F*rom time to time it's fun to close your eyes,
   and in that dark say to yourself,
"I am the sorcerer, and when I open my eyes
I shall see a world that I have created,
and for which I and only I
am completely responsible."
   *S*lowly then, eyelids open
        like curtains lifting stage-center.
   And sure enough,
   there's your world,
        just the way you built it.

*W*hoever wants truth and light
will find it for themselves.

When you look back on your days,
they've passed in a flash.
Time doesn't last,
and nobody here's got long to live.

*T*he only thing that shatters dreams
is compromise.

How easy it is to be compassionate
when it's yourself you see in trouble!

Care about understanding and

before you know it,
in just a few decades,
you'll have a system of thinking
that gives you answers
whenever you ask.

*Y*ou are fiction to the selves
who took other paths and choices.
They are fiction to you.

You've got a lot to learn from each other.

*T*o learn anything,
you must put aside
the safety of your ignorance.

You wait a lifetime to meet Someone
who understands you, accepts you as you are.
At the end, you find that Someone, all along,
has been you.

$\mathcal{H}$ow do you want
　　　　　to come out of this experience—
how do you want to be changed because of it?

$\mathcal{N}$o one forces you to learn.

You'll learn when you want to.

A fledgling leaps because it trusts its wings;
a lemming leaps because everybody else is doing it.

*O*ne's an adventure into new dimensions,
the other's suicide.

Why bother to live an unhappy life?

*T*he individual is always the exception.

"Everybody can't . . ."
but
anybody can.

*I*t's easy to live the expected and conventional. It's when you live the unexpected that you start having fun with your life.

What many take for realistic
is the suppression of their deepest knowing.

Why be realistic?

*B*efore you'll change,
something important must be at risk.

*I*f you don't want to be a teacher,
you'd better get off the planet.

A creative mind
makes uncommon connections.
So does a crazy mind.
A creative mind
makes uncommon *insightful* connections.

*Y*ou build lifetimes
as spiders build webs.

Lots of trials, sometimes,
to fit one strand.

*E*very event is subjective:
not what it means, that matters,
but what it means *to you*.

*T*ime cares about Becoming.

Reality cares about Is.

There's nothing to forgive
when you know you've gathered to yourself
all of your own experiences.

Why frown at those who bring
what you've asked?

*y*ou can tell a lot about a person
when you know what gives them comfort.

*Y*ou learn most

    when you play against an opponent

        who can beat you.

Hope knows
that a lovely thing is true
before it shows up
on her doorstep.

$\mathcal{Y}$ou're master of what you've lived,

artisan at what you're living,

amateur at what's next to live.

*F*ind your strength
and you become a center of pressure
that moves your time.

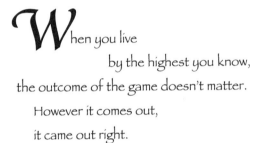

When you live
        by the highest you know,
the outcome of the game doesn't matter.

   However it comes out,

   it came out right.

*E*ven when you're brought together by
                    miraculous magnetizing,
you still have to work out problems.

A lifetime
is your chance to express the Is
in the most adventurous creative way
you can imagine.

*T*hat which most concerns and worries you—

your survival—

is the only certainty you have.

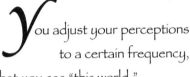ou adjust your perceptions
to a certain frequency,
and call what you see "this world."
You can tune yourself to other frequencies
whenever you wish.

*T*he creative, loving-something life
is also the healthy one.
There is healing and protection
in doing what makes you happy.

*T*he first step

        in de-hypnotizing yourself

           is to realize

that you've been hypnotized in the first place.

$\mathcal{N}$o heavens,

no hells,

just these endless worlds

you create

till you think

you've got it right.

Master's Certificate

This is to certify that the bearer has been declared a Master of Spacetime, and is authorized to command absolute control over all personal life events and an indefinite number of simultaneous life experiences, to focus consciousness among them at will, to freely choose triumph or tragedy as she or he wishes, and to magnetize such like spirits as she or he desires for her or his personal education and entertainment. This certificate is subject to the following limits: _Self-imposed_ .

It's there,
that certificate,
in everybody's pocket.

*T*here is nothing
to which you cannot give your consent,
there is nothing from which you cannot withdraw it.

Guarantee for a difficult and happy lifetime:

1. Find what you love to do
    more than anything else
    in all the world.

2. Do it,
    no matter what stands
    in your way.

3. Give the gifts of what you've learned
    from that love
    to others
    who care enough to ask.

*I*s it real? Yes, if:

it always has been,

it always will be, and,

it exists in and beyond

every corner of every alternate universe.

*I*f you want to meet someone
who can fix any situation you don't like,
who can bring you happiness
in spite of what other people say or believe,
look in a mirror,
then say this magic word:

"Hello."

$\mathcal{Y}$ou are led,

when you share your loves,
to an enchanted life of inner happiness,
which unsharing others cannot know.

*W*hen you give sparingly,
sparingly are you rewarded.
When you give worlds,
you are rewarded vastly.

*Y*our highest right knows all futures.

As you listen to its whisper,

you'll find that the prize ahead

is your own greatest happiness.

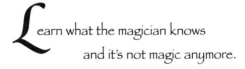

Learn what the magician knows
and it's not magic anymore.

You may not be aware,
but you know.

*W*hatever harm you would do to another,
do first to yourself.

$\mathcal{L}$ ive enough

of what you've always dreamed of doing,
    and there's no room left for feeling bad.

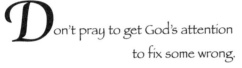

Don't pray to get God's attention
to fix some wrong.
Pray to get your own attention,
and realize that nothing needs fixing.

*Y*our mission is the luminous path that you follow,
no matter how dark the night around you.

*T*o any question,
imagine the most outlandish opposite
of the expected answer.

*I*s that one true?

*S*ome say suffer,

     some say serve,

       some say detach.

Who says find your highest right for yourself?

*T*here's nothing here but perfect.
Perfect expression of perfect life:
can't be changed,
no different truth.

*D*ying out of bodies, remember,
is as much a dream as living in them.

*L*earning is finding out what you already know.

    Doing is demonstrating that you know it.

Teaching is reminding others

        that they know just as well as you.

*Y*ou are all learners, doers, teachers.

$\mathcal{N}$ot being known

　　　　doesn't stop the truth from being true.

*Y*ou are free to smile
in the midst of massive tests and challenges,
knowing that you have chosen to play this game,
and that you have dominion
over all the appearances of earth.

*T*he simplest questions are the most profound.

Where were you born? Where is your home?
Where are you going? What are you doing?

*T*hink about these once in a while, and
watch your answers change.

$\mathcal{M}$ortalhood is a fine state to visit,

but you'd better not call it home.

*E*very person,
all the events of your life
are there because you have drawn them there.

*W*hat you choose to do with them
is up to you.

If it's got atoms, it isn't real.

$\mathcal{Y}$ou teach best

what you most need to learn.

*L*ive never to be ashamed
if anything you do or say
is published around the world—
even if what is published is not true.

*Y*our friends will know you better
in the first minute you meet
than your acquaintances will know you in
a thousand years.

*T*he Is
is Life, Love, the Magnificent IT
at the center of your being.

The Is does not recognize the limitations of spacetime,
nor does it recognize your sorrows, fears, or beliefs.

It does not see you as an upright biped
on the surface of a third planet
from a little sun
at the edge of a small galaxy
of an insignificant universe
sandwiched for a moment between
multiple trillions of other universes.

It sees you reflecting Itself,
and allows you the absolute freedom
to do anything you wish,
except to die.

*T*o bring anything into your life,
imagine that it's already there.

*D*isaster is change.

It's opportunity in a loose-fitting, hooded garment.

$\mathcal{T}$he best way to avoid responsibility is to say,

"I've got responsibilities."

*L*isten to your answers even when they're mad,
so long as they're your highest truth.

*Y*ou are free
   to change your level of consciousness
      by whim, learning, or design.

*Y*ou are not free
   to stop expressing life.

*T*he bond that links your true family
is not one of blood,
but of respect and joy in each other's life.

*R*arely do members of one family grow up
under the same roof.

*Y*ou are led

        through your lifetime

        by the inner learning creature,

the playful spiritual being that is your real self.

    Don't turn away from possible futures

    before you're certain you don't have

    anything to learn from them.

*Y*ou're always free

        to change your mind

        and choose a different future,

    or a different past.

*A*rgue for your limitations,
and sure enough,
they're yours.

*I*t is easy to forget your times of knowing,
to think they've been dreams
or old miracles, one time.

*N*othing good is a miracle,
nothing lovely is a dream.

Don't believe what your eyes are telling you.
All they show is limitation.
Look with your understanding,
find out what you already know,
and you'll see the way to fly.

*T*here's no disaster
        that can't become a blessing,
and no blessing
that can't become a disaster.

*T*he world
is your exercise-book, the pages
on which you do your sums.

*I*t is not reality,
although you can express reality
there if you wish.

You are also
free to write nonsense,
or lies, or to tear
the pages.

*L*isten to your life.

It's showing you everything you need to know
about who you can become.

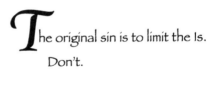

The original sin is to limit the Is.
Don't.

*Y*our character grows
from following your highest sense of right,
from trusting ideals
without being sure they'll work.

There is no such thing as a problem without a gift for you in its hands. You seek problems because you need their gifts.

*O*ne challenge of your adventure on earth
     is to rise above dead systems:
    wars, religions, nations, destructions—
    to refuse to be a part of them,
    and express instead
    the highest self

                you know how to be.

A cloud does not know
why it moves in just such a
direction and at such a speed.
It feels an impulsion. . . . This is the place to go now.

B ut the sky knows
the reasons and the patterns
behind all clouds, and you will know, too,
when you lift yourself high enough
to see beyond horizons.

*I*f you will practice being fictional for a while, you will understand that fictional characters are sometimes more real than people with bodies and heartbeats.

*Y*our conscience is the measure
    of the honesty of your selfishness.
Listen to it carefully.

*T*he truth you speak
has no past and no future.

It is,

and that's all it needs to be.

*D*estiny doesn't push you
where you don't want to go.

You're the one who chooses.

Destiny's up to you.

You are a creature of light.
From light have you come,
to light shall you go,
and surrounding you through every step
is the light of your infinite being.

*I*magine the universe beautiful and just and

perfect. Then be sure of one thing:

The Is has imagined it

quite a bit better than you have.

Do unto others
as you truly feel
like doing unto others.

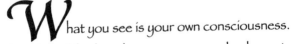

What you see is your own consciousness.
When that's lifted up, how your scenes do change!

*H*ere's a test
    to find whether your mission on earth
    is finished:

      *I*f you're alive, it isn't.

*A*void problems
and you'll never be the one who overcame them.

$\mathcal{D}$on't be dismayed at good-byes.
A farewell is necessary before you can meet again.
And meeting again, after moments or lifetimes,
is certain for those who are friends.

*Y*ou have the power to do anything you wish
except these two:

You cannot create reality.
You cannot destroy it.

*W*hen will you learn
to expect what you can't imagine
will happen?

You are never given a wish

  without also being given

  the power to make it true.

You may have to work for it, however.

How others deal with gifts you've given
is not your decision, but theirs.

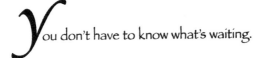

You don't have to know what's waiting.

You're guided by your highest right,
and wherever it takes you
is where you need to go.

*S*ometimes you'd best keep quiet about
what you know.

Fast as light within,

but outside, let's take her

one step at a time.

*Y*our religion
is your way
of finding what is true.

The only thing that matters,
   at the end of a stay on earth, is

How well did you love?
What was the quality of your love?

*T*here are no mistakes.
The events you bring upon yourself,
no matter how unpleasant,
are necessary in order to learn
what you need to learn.

*W*hatever step you take,
it's necessary to reach the place
you've chosen to go.

*Y*ou gave your life
     to become the person you are right now.

*W*as it worth it?

*L*ife Is.

That's where you go for
healing, comfort, energy, perspective.

*O*ne way to pick a future is to believe it's inevitable.

*T*o name a thing
is harmless.

To name ideas

is to create a religion.

Don't you dare!

*Y*ou've held to your sense of right,
your inner ethics,
even when it's been hard or dangerous
or when others call you strange.

*T*hat strangeness sets you apart;
it makes you lonely.
What are you going to do about that?

*T*he Is doesn't need you to tell anybody
how it works.

The mark of your ignorance
is the depth of your belief in injustice and tragedy.

What the caterpillar calls the end of the world,
the master calls a butterfly.

You are all.
Free.
To do.
Whatever.
You want.
To do.

*I*n order to live free and happily,
you must sacrifice boredom.

It is not always an easy
sacrifice.

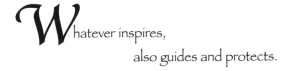

Whatever inspires,

also guides and protects.

K

now that ever about
you stands the reality of love,
and each moment
you have the power
to transform your world
by what you have learned.

*Y*our oneness in love
is reality,
and mirages
cannot change reality.

*D*on't forget. No matter what seems to be.

*B*elieve you know all answers,
and you know all answers.
Believe you're a master
and you are one.

No one can solve problems
for someone whose problem is
that they don't want
their problems solved.

You don't have to fight
to live as you wish.
Live as you wish
and pay whatever price is required.

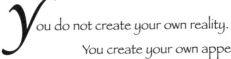

You do not create your own reality.

You create your own appearances.

Big difference!

*A*ny principle that requires admiration isn't real.
Any God who requires worship doesn't exist.

Who you are is someone
who asked to be dropped off on earth
so you could do something remarkable,
something that matters to you,
which you could not do anywhere, anywhen else.

The only way to win, sometimes, is to surrender.

*S*acrifice is giving up something you want
for something you don't want.

*I*t is never required.

*T*ake your dying with some seriousness.
To be delighted on the way to your death
is not generally understood
by less-advanced life-forms, and they'll
call you crazy.

*E*verything in this book may be wrong.

MARY MAGDALENE, BELOVED DISCIPLE
Clysta Kinstler

This beautifully written book is far more than a novel. It is a healing visualisation which restores women and the Divine Feminine to their rightful place in our inner world. Told movingly through Mary's eyes, this powerful tale blends together illuminating insights into the *Hieros Gamos* or Sacred Marriage, the ritual re-enactment of the story of Isis and Osiris, and the mysteries of goddess worship. Though 'only' a novel, **Mary Magdalene, Beloved Disciple** strikes a deep chord of truth. Whatever your beliefs, you will enjoy it!

334pp, 138mm x 216mm, softback, 2005, RRP £9.95
Code: 151103 Cygnus Price £6.55

www.cygnus-books.co.uk

THE DIAMOND
IN YOUR POCKET

Discovering Your True Radiance

GANGAJI

FOREWORD BY ECKHART TOLLE

THE DIAMOND IN YOUR POCKET Gangaji

Gangaji is an American-born teacher who, with her radiant presence and gentle encouragement, has shown thousands of people how simple it is to step through the endless chatter of their minds and enter the silent, utterly peaceful brilliance at the core of their being. She shows you how to experience consciously the motionless, yet endlessly powerful hub of your own being, so that the whole movement of your life can be informed by it. As Gangaji explains, this doesn't mean that your life will be swept clean of conflicts, challenges, pain or suffering. It means that you will have recognized a sanctuary, where the truth of yourself is present, where limitless peace is present, regardless of the physical, mental, or emotional circumstances of your life. Having recognized this sanctuary, even momentarily, what then? Can we stay in it? Or must we inevitably lose contact with it again, as we are swept along in the relentless tide of everyday life? Gangaji answers this question, too, with deep and liberating wisdom. Foreword by *Eckhart Tolle.*

280pp, 150mm x 230mm, softback, 2006
Publisher's Edition RRP £15.99
Code: 160404 Cygnus Prices: 1 copy £7.65
2-10 copies £7.15 each, 11+ copies £6.95 each

Call Cygnus on 0845 456 1577

THE GENTLE ART OF BLESSING
Pierre Pradervand

Mystics tell us that behind the veil of material appearances exists an infinite, unconditionally loving principle of benevolence, abundance and peace. Would you like to develop your own awareness of that? An awareness so vivid, so unwavering that you can no longer mistake the veil for the reality? An awareness so penetrating that the laws of Love, with their transforming, healing power, are admitted even into the darkest hell? This, and no less, is the aim of **The Gentle Art of Blessing**, described so eloquently by Pierre Pradervand. **The Gentle Art of Blessing** is the perfect way to develop an awareness constantly centred in love, even in the midst of trying circumstances. When you make it your daily spiritual practice, it will be impossible for your heart not to expand. From a narrow cubicle, it will become a temple without walls.

295pp, 127mm x 202mm, softback, 2004, RRP £10.95

Code: 140801 Cygnus Prices: 1 copy £6.95
2-10 copies £6.50 each, 11+ copies £6.30 each

www.cygnus-books.co.uk

SUMMER WITH THE LEPRECHAUNS
Tanis Helliwell

Summer with the Leprechauns describes a summer Tanis Helliwell spent in an old Irish country cottage. Sensitive to subtle energies, Tanis found the cottage occupied by a leprechaun who was intent on making contact with her. A deep communication ensued, in which the leprechaun passed on powerful teachings, some of which we have rarely read about elsewhere. How may we help elementals in their evolution? How can we work with our 'body elemental'? Can elementals and humans work together in new ways? These questions and many others are answered in this wonderful book, which admits us to the secrets of the fairy realm.

206pp, 138mm x 216mm, softback, 2005
Publisher's Edition RRP £9.99
Code: 150303 Cygnus Price £5.00

Call Cygnus on 0845 456 1577